FRENCH
cottage

FRENCH
cottage

FROM THE PUBLISHERS OF

the cottage® journal MAGAZINE

FRENCH cottage

PRESIDENT/CCO Brian Hart Hoffman
VICE PRESIDENT/EDITORIAL Cindy Smith Cooper
ART DIRECTOR Stephanie Lambert

EDITORIAL
EDITOR Linda Baltzell Wright
CREATIVE DIRECTOR/PHOTOGRAPHY Mac Jamieson
ASSOCIATE EDITOR Katie Wood
EDITORIAL COORDINATOR Mary-Kate Sherer
COPY EDITOR Whitney Durrwachter
CONTRIBUTING WRITERS
Annalise DeVries, Avery Hurt, Vicki Ingham, Robert C. Martin,
Stacey Norwood, Kathryn Renner, Tovah Martin
CONTRIBUTING STYLIST Yukie McLean
SENIOR PHOTOGRAPHERS John O'Hagan,
Marcy Black Simpson
PHOTOGRAPHERS
Jim Bathie, William Dickey, Stephanie Welbourne
ASSISTANT PHOTOGRAPHER Caroline Smith
CONTRIBUTING PHOTOGRAPHERS
Stephen DeVries, Joanne Holloway
SENIOR DIGITAL IMAGING SPECIALIST Delisa McDaniel
DIGITAL IMAGING SPECIALIST Clark Densmore

hm | books

CHAIRMAN OF THE BOARD/CEO Phyllis Hoffman DePiano
PRESIDENT/COO Eric W. Hoffman
PRESIDENT/CCO Brian Hart Hoffman
EXECUTIVE VICE PRESIDENT/CFO Mary P. Cummings
EXECUTIVE VICE PRESIDENT/ OPERATIONS & MANUFACTURING Greg Baugh
VICE PRESIDENT/DIGITAL MEDIA Jon Adamson
VICE PRESIDENT/EDITORIAL Cindy Smith Cooper
VICE PRESIDENT/ADMINISTRATION Lynn Lee Terry

Sign up for *The Cottage Journal's* newsletter at *thecottagejournal.com*.

EDITORIAL & ADVERTISING SALES OFFICES
1900 International Park Drive, Suite 50, Birmingham, AL 35243
Phone: 205-995-8860, 888-411-8995   Fax: 205-380-2740
Website: *thecottagejournal.com*

CUSTOMER SERVICE
The Cottage Journal, P.O. Box 6201, Harlan, IA 51593
Phone: 888-393-6246   E-mail: CJScustserv@cdsfulfillment.com

Copyright © 2016 by Hoffman Media

All rights reserved. No part of this book may be reproduced or transmitted in any form or
by any means, electronic or mechanical, including photocopying, or by any information
storage and retrieval system, without permission in writing from Hoffman Media.
Reviewers may quote brief passages for specific inclusion in a magazine or newspaper.

Hoffman Media
1900 International Park Drive, Suite 50
Birmingham, Alabama 35243
www.hoffmanmedia.com

ISBN # 978-1-940772-28-8
Printed in China.

CONTENTS

INTRODUCTION

The love of French style is most often described as "love at first sight," discovered either while touring in France or seeing a home in the style. The distinction of the Parisian style is the added layers of charm with elegant vintage furnishings or the lovely vignettes and accessories. French antiques from the 1940s and earlier generally influence the style, and decorating with vintage designer furniture, French leather books, couture clothing, musical instruments, and fine linens adds a subtle touch of style to the home.

From the inspiration of the country cottage with relaxed furniture and rustic paint finishes to the romantic cottage style with its soft color palettes and small outdoor gardens of ivy with cobblestone paths and vine-covered walkways, the look is always inviting.

Your home should reflect your personality, so include your own keepsakes when decorating. A family heirloom or painting might blend with an antique or flea market piece, giving a timeless sort of mix to your style. In the pages of this book, you will find French accents found from treasure hunts and markets that make classic, French style come to life in your home.

chapter 1

FRENCH HOME DÉCOR

———————————

COMFORTABLE ELEGANCE

THESE HOMEOWNERS TASTEFULLY SHOWCASE THEIR LOVE OF
HUNTING IN THEIR COMFORTABLY CRAFTED COTTAGE.

When Mark and Nancy Peeples built their cozy cottage nearly 12 years ago, they designed it with the mountains in mind. "My husband loves the West, the mountains, and hunting," Nancy says. "So we were trying to have some sort of comfortable, elegant version of that."

Their charming cottage exterior is sided with hand-split cedar shakes and is unlike any of the homes in their neighborhood. "We've got a real mountain retreat in the middle of the city," she laughs.

The couple's enchanting abode exudes an upscale elegance while still maintaining personal touches. With the help of interior designer Mary Finch, Nancy outfitted her home with one-of-a-kind salvaged finds and antiques from around the world. The great room stands tall beneath the house's A-frame, and reclaimed beams help draw the eye upward. The limestone fireplace with detailed crest work and an antique tapestry anchor the large room with a European flair. Across from the fireplace a collection of European mounts reflects Mark's love for game hunting in a way that feels polished and refined.

Just two steps up from the great room brings you into the dining room, which expertly balances a space that is cozy and intimate for special meals but also open and connected to the main living area. The family of four spends lots of time in their dreamy, light-filled kitchen. Whether they're entertaining or enjoying a quiet morning, there are plenty of spaces to unwind and relax at the kitchen's island bar or custom-built French Country banquette. "I love to cook, and I love to entertain," Nancy says. "Our kitchen has definitely been the center of our house."

Like moths to a flame groups tend to flock to small, inviting spaces in the home. Mark, Nancy, and their two daughters can typically be found visiting together not in the great room but in the tiny den off the master bedroom. "We built it small thinking it would be just Mark and I, but it ends up being the place for all four of us." Nancy shares. "It's one of my favorite areas of the home; the den with the little fireplace—that's our hub."

Since Mark and Nancy built their home from the ground up, they got to have a say in most design choices. And for Nancy, her vision was simple. "It had to be very comfortable. You had to be able to put your feet on everything," she says, noting her home enjoys a constant flow of traffic and she wanted things to be beautiful but approachable. "[My home] is very open, inviting, and casual but still feels elegant. Every room had to have that flavor."

A cozy den is always a favorite gathering spot.

The island and counters in the kitchen make
conversation easy among the family.

"My home is very open, inviting, and casual but still feels elegant. Every room had to have that flavor." —NANCY PEEPLES

RUSTIC
FRENCH STYLE

THIS COZY KITCHEN IS A REFLECTION OF THE CREATIVE
PASSIONS OF BOTH HUSBAND AND WIFE.

Creating a home is like making a delicious meal. Sometimes the perfect blend of ingredients looks like a hodgepodge on a shopping list, but after just one bite of the expertly blended flavors of the finished dish, no one can deny the incredible taste. The same can be said for Ben and Ginny Smith's cottage style.

The Smiths' kitchen is a mix of both Ben and Ginny. Ben is a craftsman and avid hunter while Ginny is an antiques dealer with a love for all things French. The couple had been toying with the idea of redoing their tiny kitchen space to better accommodate their family of three small boys, but it was Ginny who finally pulled the trigger. "My husband went hunting, and he came home and saw that I had taken a crow bar and a sledgehammer and gutted the whole kitchen," she recalls with a laugh. They later knocked down the wall that separated the kitchen from the living room to maximize their space.

Luckily the couple makes a great team and creatively found ways to design a custom kitchen they both could enjoy. "We had to have a little bit of my world and a little bit of his world," Ginny says of the kitchen style, which is reflected in nearly every vignette. With the help of Ginny's decorator sister Mallory of Mallory Smith Interiors, the French antiques, gilt, and gold for Ginny now pair beautifully with the rustic barnwood, antlers, and ironwork for Ben. "It wasn't a certain look that we were going for," Ginny says but rather a collection of inspiration that worked in the space. "Plus, we have three little boys so we want to keep it as comfortable as possible."

Perhaps the most impressive thing about this rustic Old-World kitchen is that Ben made everything from the barnwood countertops and cabinets to the iron chandeliers

and oven hood. "He's got great taste," Ginny says. "I would be in France or away from home, and he would be working on pieces and send me pictures. I'd come home and he had just done it!"

Because each piece was handmade and tailored to fit the Smiths' lifestyle and passions, nearly everything in the kitchen has a story. The island, for example, was built with pieces of wood from fallen trees at Ben's hunting property, and the countertops are made from pieces of wood they found in a barn. The cabinet doors on each side of the sink were found in France. They were falling apart, so Ben made hinges that go all the way across and actually hold the door together, making them fully functional for daily use.

While the space is beautiful, timeworn, and one-of-a-kind, Ginny says the most important thing to her was "just keeping it where the boys could live in it, and if they messed things up, it would actually look better."

Behind the range sits a beautiful French antique made of wood and plaster. Ginny found the piece on a shopping trip in France; it is an old built-in piece that came out of a home in the South of France.

"We had to have a little bit of my world and a little bit of his world."

—GINNY SMITH

VINTAGE
FRENCH CHARM

HARKING BACK TO AN ERA WHEN EVERYDAY OBJECTS WERE CRAFTED TO
LAST, EUROPEAN GRAIN SACKS PROVIDED THE PALETTE AND INSPIRATION FOR
TIM AND BRENDA DEWITT'S UNASSUMINGLY ELEGANT GUEST COTTAGE.

When she spotted the feed sacks at an antiques market, Brenda DeWitt knew she
had found the centerpiece for her guest cottage named Chelsea Cottage. "I wanted
the space to be beautiful and durable. I wanted guests with children and dogs to feel
comfortable," she says. "That is why I love feed sacks—they are sturdy yet inviting."

Repurposed as curtains, pillowcases, and lamp shades and used in the dog bed that Brenda created, they are just one example of her eye for the possible. After she and her husband, Tim, purchased their 1940s bungalow, they tore down a dilapidated detached garage in the backyard to make room for a guest cottage and an oak-shaded courtyard. Now, the welcoming retreat houses a trove of found objects and salvaged furniture that echoes the soft and subtle reds of the feed sacks and makes the place feel like home.

Whether she was distressing the front door to achieve the perfect patina or reupholstering armchairs she bought for a song, Brenda realized with her own two hands the charm she was seeking. The DeWitts did most of the work themselves—from drawing up blueprints to building the countertops and hanging the tongue-and-groove walls.

An oak-shaded courtyard, where friends can enjoy a meal while seated around a zinc-topped farmhouse table, showcases the homeowners' handiwork. Tim fashioned the gate out of lumber left over from the cottage's construction, and Brenda laid the Tennessee flagstone underfoot.

Appreciating the scale of the surrounding neighborhood, composed of quaint bungalows, Brenda and Tim chose to build a two-room cottage rather than add a guest room onto their own home. Fifteen-foot ceilings and large casement windows create an open and spacious setting. Light mingles with an eclectic collection Brenda has garnered on countless mornings spent at yard sales, flea markets, and antiques shops.

European linens are among the finest in the world, with the French producing some of the whitest and most delicate of textiles.

Because of the couple's hands-on approach, no corner of the 20x20-foot structure is wasted, and each design decision sings with purpose. A plate rack displays and stores the dishes guests use during their stays, for example, and an old metal washbasin finds new life as a sink.

"The floors are pine, so they will age beautifully. I like things that are worn but lasting," Brenda notes. "I don't care if dogs run across the floor or if a friend in high heels scuffs it—that gives a place character. I love the imperfections."

The pine floors and found pieces bestow upon the cottage a cozy warmth, while the linens, high ceilings, and large casement windows keep the space open and airy.

"For me, a cottage should be a sanctuary," Brenda says with a smile. "When the outside world is crazy, we need somewhere peaceful to go."

An old shelf gets new life with a simple gray wash.
Antique linens and quilts find a home on an armoire.

"For me, a cottage should be a sanctuary. When the outside world is crazy, we need somewhere peaceful to go." —BRENDA DEWITT

The monogram on the pillows is that of Chelsea Jerome, Tim and Brenda's first dog and the cottage's namesake. A white palette with red accents ties together the room's furniture, linens, and decorative items.

WHERE GRACEFUL SHADOWS FALL

ANTICIPATE THE WHIMS AND WISHES OF GUESTS WITH A GRACIOUS
COTTAGE FILLED WITH ROMANTIC FRENCH TOUCHES.

When decorating a cottage for guests to enjoy or for you to escape to on special weekends, it is important to consider every detail. A beautiful bathroom with special amenities makes guests feel pampered. A bedroom becomes inviting and warm with extra blankets, the luxurious feel of crisp clean sheets, pens and paper, and books or movies to curl up and enjoy. It's the little things that make a big difference during a special weekend getaway.

Clever touches and sweet surprises make stay-over visitors feel especially welcome. The graceful headboard and delicate boudoir chairs incorporate French style.

An inviting, sunny seating area for reclining and relaxing is essential. Place books and periodicals within easy reach of a comfy sofa and chair.

The walls are bathed in white to reflect the natural light that
streams into this guest cottage. Wood furniture pieces are painted in
soothing colors and accented with delicate, romantic designs.

A special breakfast nook with a small table, comfortable chairs upholstered in lovely coordinating fabrics, tiny lamps, and exquisite china is an enjoyable spot for meals.

"*A guest
never
forgets the
host who
had treated
him kindly.*"

—HOMER

The owners have paid attention to
every detail—including amenities
you might find in a top hotel.
Fragrant soaps, lovely fresh linens,
and other thoughtful touches
invite guests to unwind and enjoy
a soothing soak in the bathroom.
To make the cottage feel more like
home, the host family thoughtfully
chose each painting, print, and
knickknack at a special place.
Fluffy white linens and plush robes
are simple things that make guests
feel welcome.

And don't forget about the grounds. Climbing vines and sunny
blossoms keep the garden relaxed and carefree.

PICTURE PERFECT

WHITE WALLS MAKE AN IDEAL CANVAS FOR
A COLLAGE OF ANTIQUE FINDS.

As a professional photographer, Heather Cummans knows that the first shot—the initial impression—can speak volumes about the subject of a portrait. That's why curb appeal, that great first look, became Heather's top priority when she moved into her cozy cottage seven years ago.

"It didn't take much work to spruce up the front of the house," Heather recalls. "In fact, I was surprised what a difference just a little money and time could make." A white picket fence, pale painted shutters, and planted flower boxes added color and quaintness to the facade while Mother Nature completed the inviting look with lush jasmine, boxwood, and ivy.

Inside, Heather worked with the home's assets and was able to limit major renovations to the kitchen. Creamy cabinetry and updated appliances are accented by treasured pieces such as an intricate ironwork accent hanging over the kitchen sink.

After graduating with a degree in interior design from The Art Institute of Atlanta, Heather studied 19th-century decorative arts at Sotheby's in London. While there, her love for romantic French style bloomed, inspiring a number of collections that Heather has added to over the years. Well-curated groupings of art, china, angels, and books peek out from cupboards and shelves, but the highlights of Heather's home are the treasured antiques integrated throughout each room.

Painted furniture pieces and intricate window treatments provide pops of color to contrast the home's crisp white walls. In the living room sits a painted green armchair from a restored New Orleans hotel that inspired the home's eclectic style, Heather says. Other pieces were gifted from five generations of beloved family matriarchs

while others originate from local shops to markets as far away as Budapest, Hungary.

By the front door, a sturdy, whitewashed secretary desk from Heather's great, great, great-grandmother houses frames filled with images of loved ones, as well as books and other keepsakes. Much like Heather's photography, her home is filled with moments captured in time. The pieces tell stories of bygone days, and there is plenty of room for more treasures and more picture-perfect memories to come.

By simply removing the doors from this antique secretary desk, Heather blended style and function, resulting in a pretty and practical focal point. Drawers can keep necessities in easy reach.

Add height to your home—or at least the illusion of height—with top-embellished window treatments. These striking solid panels epitomize the beauty of French cottage style.

Heather selected a clean, creamy palette for nearly the entire home. She considers her walls a subtle backdrop that allow a collection of furniture and accessories to truly steal the show.

THE JOY OF FRENCH CHARM

MUCH-LOVED ANTIQUES BESTOW CONTINENTAL APPEAL
UPON AN OPEN AND INVITING COTTAGE.

When the residents of this home moved in nearly 15 years ago, the wife couldn't have been more thrilled to have a fitting home for her beloved French antiques. A number of projects were soon underway as the couple made the cozy cottage their own. A complete kitchen redesign opened up the space for cooking and entertaining, while the master bath was decked with a striking pair of pedestal sinks and antique mirrors.

One of the homeowners' favorite aspects of their abode is the pleasing view of the carriage house from the breakfast room.

This French-inspired kitchen is as versatile as it is functional. Dappled with a blend of French antiques, collections, and personal touches, this comforatble kitchen is where the homeowners spend most of their time.

This contemporary dining table made of wooden dowels has been a conversation piece in each of the couple's homes. The wife says she simply changes out the chairs to fit the new home's style. Rather than focus on large clutter-prone collections, this homeowner prefers to purchase special pieces she particularly enjoys, such as this charming piggy cookie jar and salt-and-pepper set.

Simple design selections like the white shutters flanking the master bed combine with decorative fixtures and lamps to add both height and light to the couple's suite.

LE PETIT CHATEAU

THERE WAS NO QUESTION ABOUT THE ARCHITECTURAL STYLE WHEN THIS COUPLE BEGAN PLANNING TO BUILD A SECOND HOME BY THE LAKE. IT HAD TO BE FRENCH.

Frances Stanford fell in love with the French language and culture in high school and college. "The first time I was in Paris, I felt like I already knew [the city]," she says. After her children were grown, she and her daughter opened an antiques store. On regular buying trips to Europe, they roamed all over the French countryside, gathering antiques and building friendships. Naturally, once the house project was underway, they shopped for period doors, gates, architectural elements, chandeliers, furniture, and accessories for the new home.

French Country style is surprisingly well adapted to the Southern climate, at least the way architect Chris Reebals interpreted it. Steeply pitched ceilings, thick-stucco walls, limestone floors, and well-placed windows and doors encourage natural cooling, and a courtyard and porch invite indoor–outdoor living. Salvaged beams and barn-board ceilings add an Old-World look that suits the antique furnishings. "We handpicked every beam," Frances says.

Building and decorating the house was a family affair. Her son-in-law did much of the construction himself, including building all of the arches and custom doorframes and hand-forging replicas of missing door hinges. He even sketched out the French Country range hood in the kitchen and built it on the spot.

Frances turned the decorating over to her other daughter. To complement the 18th- and 19th-century furnishings, she chose comfortable upholstered seating covered in durable pretreated fabrics that can easily stand up to spills and wet bathing suits. The house has become a beloved family gathering spot for holidays and summer vacations. "We have three children, all married, and eight grandchildren," Frances says. "The house is very comfortable for everyone."

The basket atop the Louis XV vaisselier (dresser), right, is a grape-harvest basket designed to be carried by a donkey.

"The first time I was in Paris, I felt like I already knew the city."

—FRANCES STANFORD

Mutton-bone chairs from the early 19th century encourage lingering after dinner at the long antique dining table. Frances says the confit pots in the corner cupboard were originally used to store cooked duck.

Antique doors, sconces, and storage pieces give Old-World character to every room in the house—from the entry all the way to the grandchildren's room at the end of the house. Son-in-law Ben Smith worked with blacksmith Derek Weldon to create the custom stair rail in the entry.

NATURE AND LIGHT

TWO ARTISTS FIND A HOME THAT PROPELS THEIR CREATIVITY IN THE SECLUSION OF THE SOUTHWESTERN COUNTRYSIDE.

Light dances atop the row of lavender planted along the back terrace, beckoning one to linger for a moment, breathe deeply, and soak up the natural beauty of the surrounding French countryside. The accompanying house sets a welcoming tone, as its pale walls, sloping roof, and central turret conjure up a sense of storybook whimsy. Certainly for owners Edward and Heather Cowie, this home in the Dordogne region of southwestern France enriches and encourages the imagination.

As artists, Edward and Heather have found a place entrenched in its natural setting where they can freely express their creativity. "We couldn't be happy living in a house that wasn't connected to nature," Edward explains. As a painter and composer, Edward built his studio next to the neighboring woodland, allowing him to peer out of the windows and see the trees and nearby valley.

Heather, a former geologist, keeps her paints, pastels, and other media in the basement, where light streams in to reveal a warm and cozy space. "It's sort of a nesting feeling when I'm down there," she says. "As though the earth is wrapped around me."

From the light and scenery pouring into the house through French doors and windows to the families of birds nesting in the eaves, the Cowies' home is inseparable from its landscape. "All of our artwork revolves around the natural world," Heather says. "So having a house that's lived in by other creatures is actually a real thrill."

As the couple sees it, the house itself is a work of art. "I fell in love with the form of the house because it's very sculptural," Edward explains.

"It's like living in a sculpture."

—HEATHER COWIE

To complement the curves and angles of the house's form, the Cowies' decorative choices focus on clean lines and neutral tones, allowing the structure to remain the central showpiece. From there, they have filled shelves and accented tabletops with items found on their travels.

"It's just awe-inspiring—the colors of the earth." —HEATHER COWIE

With the kitchen opening up onto a large terrace, the Cowies' home provides the perfect setting for Heather to work on the creation of handcrafted silk ribbon.

Like a naturalist's collection of unique objects, her neatly arranged pebbles and bones—found while exploring the outdoors—accompany the many pencils and paints in the studio.

For Edward, music and painting are inseparable art forms. The movement of sound carries a visual quality, he explains, so that the audible experience connects to color and form.

The home incorporates "the memorabilia of our lives," Heather explains, featuring items collected from their world travels, paintings inspired by different places, and items treasured for years, including a piano from 1805, which Edward says, "we've carted around the world."

EDGEWOOD COTTAGE

ENTERTAINING INSPIRED A FRENCH KITCHEN REMODEL
AND GREW THROUGHOUT THIS QUAINT HOME.

Two small rooms located on the back of this tiny cottage were combined into a
lovely room for entertaining friends—namely favorite neighbors that drop in daily
and chat while dinner is being prepared in the open kitchen. Ceiling heights were
raised for additional natural light in the room, and storage with open shelving is

handsomely displayed with a homemade pottery collection. Soft accents of seafoam paint were used on several cabinets, giving just a hint of color. The reclaimed paned doors in the hallway were brushed with seafoam to echo the patina from the color palette in the kitchen.

The welcoming porch adds harmony to the cottage as well with vintage wicker and a settee made from an antique bed. The lower ceiling heights in the front rooms add to the home's quaint charm. As you enter the kitchen area, natural light fills the room with additional ceiling height. It has understandably become the favorite home for friends to gather.

Gilt chandeliers are the pièce de résistance in each small room, with French doors opening to each bedroom. Layers of collected linens and plenty of pillows invite guests to relax and comfortably rest with ease.

Groupings of candle holders and brown and taupe
transferware delight the eye in the dining room.

Clever use of door hardware, washed with paint and used as knobs
(left), adds a French flair, as does the wire basket for linens.

Costume jewelry, belonging to the homeowner's grandmother, souvenirs, and vintage accessories are gathered for display as objects of art on antique mannequins. French hats are treated as jewels of artwork and are amusing to the eye.

FRENCH
ELEGANCE

THE PATINATED CHARM OF FRENCH COUNTRY DESIGN IS TIMELESS.
COMBINING IT WITH AN OPEN-CONCEPT FLOOR PLAN MAKES FOR
THE BEST OF BOTH WORLDS FOR THESE HOMEOWNERS.

When home builder Scott Thomson asked homeowners Tom and Kay Worley what they wanted in their new home Kay was ready with answers. "I want light and lots of windows. I want nooks and crannies, places for my books, and a garden I can see from my kitchen window," Kay says. "And that's where we started." Scott sketched three plans, and Kay and decorator Pandy Agnew kept tweaking them until a plan was in motion.

Kay had always loved French Country design for what she calls its "softness." This decorating style is identified with curving lines, chandeliers, and antiques yet is still known for being comfortable. Achieving this feeling in a brand-new home with an open floor plan isn't easy, but Pandy's talent and Scott's vision proved successful.

Neutrals usually override color in French Country style, and Pandy followed suit. A favorite painting by artist Emily Ozier that hung in the kitchen of the Worleys' previous home and now hangs above the table proved to be the perfect palette for color choices for the new interiors. Soft French blues with lots of neutrals were picked for furnishings and fabrics, and the walls in the home were veiled in a warm cream.

White oak was selected for the flooring in most rooms. "I've learned from my own house that light floors are easier to keep," Pandy explained. "They don't fade as easily." However, in the dining room they opted for travertine tile but kept the color light for a subtle transition between rooms.

As a member of two book clubs, book storage has become an issue for Kay, so built-in bookcases were created on the stair landing and also in the dining room surrounding the French doors, which lead to the newly planted garden. The garden includes romantic European elements like a fountain and a woven-willow fence. And the most perfect thing about the space is that Kay can see it from her kitchen window.

With all the wants checked off the list, the homeowners can now revel in the delight of an inviting home sure to charm family and friends.

True to French Country style, timeworn elements complement soft, inviting pieces. The original limestone fireplace and rustic beams complement the delicate linens on the furniture, bringing interest to the space.

With lightly colored floors and creamy white walls as a canvas, Pandy was able to fill the living room with Kay's beloved antiques.

Natural light pouring in through the French doors makes the crystal chandelier shine while the dark wood dining table and chairs provide a stark contrast to the light and airy room.

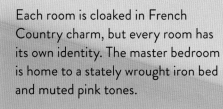

Each room is cloaked in French Country charm, but every room has its own identity. The master bedroom is home to a stately wrought iron bed and muted pink tones.

chapter 2

FRENCH GARDEN CHARM

———————————

GARDEN ROOMS

FURNISHED WITH FLOWERING VINES, EVERGREEN SHRUBS, AND WELL-PLACED CONTAINERS, OUTDOOR SPACES BECOME INTIMATE, WELCOMING ROOMS THAT ARE AS PERFECT FOR PARTIES AS THEY ARE FOR TRANQUIL RELAXATION.

Inspired by country villas in France's Provence region, the garden rooms of this lovely stucco home start with architectural elements—a terrace off the dining room, a covered walk along the front of the house, and a wall enclosing the backyard. Vines and shrubs soften these features and ease the transition into the outdoor living areas.

The garden rooms expand the home's entertaining space by drawing guests out to the terraces, loggia, and courtyard, where ivy-clad walls and neat rectangles of lawn create a feeling of privacy and intimacy. Focal points, such as a wrought iron table on the terrace and a fountain framed by towering arborvitae trees, anchor the rooms and create a sense of destination. Vines and shrubs offer fragrance as well as color and texture; roses and jasmine clothe the pergola, and rosemary hedges flank the terrace, filling the air with intoxicating perfumes.

A sheltered loggia offers the quiet tranquility of a cloister but can welcome a crowd of guests as well. Columns and walls cloaked in vines provide a songbird-friendly habitat with lots of nesting places for robins and finches.

FLOWER MARKETS

IN SMALL TOWNS AND BIG CITIES ACROSS FRANCE, OPEN-AIR MARKETS CONVERT PUBLIC SQUARES INTO FESTIVALS OF FRESH FLOWERS AND PLANTS. EVEN MARKETS THAT EMPHASIZE FOODS MAKE A PLACE FOR BLOOMS.

For the French, flowers are as essential as fresh baguettes. Open-air flower markets like this one, the Marché aux Fleurs, which is just a short stroll from the palace of Versailles, offer mixed bouquets and bunches of gorgeous cut blooms as well as potted herbs and flowering plants. Canopies held aloft by metal poles create temporary shelters for flowers and shoppers. From the plank tiers of buckets holding cut stems in clear plastic sleeves, bunches of Fuji mums, peonies, lilies, ageratum, and lisianthus beckon passersby with vivid colors and intoxicating fragrances. At another stall, potted herbs are ready for planting in kitchen gardens, which may be as simple as a container garden on a windowsill. The presence of plants is so fundamental to everyday life here that even apartment dwellers in elegant city buildings find ways to create their own gardens. The ornate iron grills that decorate windows afford the perfect opportunity to hang pots of flowers and herbs.

The presence of flowers is so fundamental to everyday life.

"The discovery of a new dish confers more happiness on humanity, than the discovery of a new star."

—Jean Anthelme Brillat-Savarin

ROOTED INHERITANCE

THE CORNAY'S FRENCH COUNTRY GARDEN BLOOMS
WITH LEGACY PLANTS FROM TWO FAMILIES IN A FRAGRANT
AND COLORFUL CELEBRATION OF HERITAGE.

It takes a special kind of person to appreciate inheriting a 100-year-old peony bush, but Dr. Cornay comes from a long line of plant enthusiasts. His maternal great-grandmother was so fond of a particular Old-English-style rose that she packed a few cuttings in her bags when she emigrated from France. His father's aunt was a founder of the Louisiana Iris Society and creator of the Katherine L. Cornay iris. So when Cornay and his wife, Elizabeth, inherited her grandmother's house and garden, he was more prepared than most to appreciate the property's wealth: a collection of perennials and native Alabama plants that Elizabeth's grandparents had lovingly developed for some 50 years.

In addition to building a new house on the site, the Cornays embarked on creating a larger garden that would integrate the old plants with new ones. It would also feature flowers and shrubs from his family home in Lafayette, Louisiana. With the help of landscape architect Jane Reed Ross, they created an informal French Country-style garden designed for strolling.

The garden is also designed to be appreciated in all seasons—and at all hours. As a physician, Cornay often doesn't get home until after dark. "I wanted things that would show up at night," he says. Abundant plantings of white and pale pink flowers and flowering shrubs ensure that even when the moon is just a sliver, the garden has an ethereal glow.

Following in his great-aunt's footsteps, Cornay has hybridized a Louisiana iris of his own. He also propagates the now hard-to-find Katherine L. Cornay iris, as well as his great-grandmother's rose and the century-old peony, which his wife's ancestors brought from Missouri. He views these as his inheritance, and to keep them from being lost, he roots cuttings and divides rootstocks and gives them to friends, family, and a nearby convent for their gardens. He says these family treasures are best preserved when they're shared.

chapter 3

FRENCH INSPIRATION & COLLECTIONS

CHERISHED
TREASURES

ANTIQUES ARE SAVED NOT ONLY FOR THEIR PRACTICAL
USES BUT ARE PRESERVED FOR A CONNECTION TO HISTORY
AND THE CRAFTSMANSHIP NEEDED TO CREATE IT.

Worn paint finishes and aging threads add character and timelessness to objects we collect. They can give a sense of strength and longevity to our homes that shiny new home pieces often cannot.

From large antiques shows to small estate sales, people like Martha Lauren who have collected over the years know what they are looking for. Martha's love of all things French goes back to several years ago when she opened a small shop specializing in linens for the home. She spent days each year with friends in small villages in the South of France. Chests, pictured at right, were found treasures decorated in shades of green, sepia, and gold. How to ship them became a challenge, but soon she was able to rely on trips made twice a year to fulfill her shop's needs and for her own cottage. In years past, the homeowner ran Martha Lauren Antique Linens and Accessories in Mountain Brook, Alabama.

Now enjoying collecting and spending time decorating her new cottage, she is focused on each room that her cherished furniture pieces will occupy.

Silver gleams in a small display case, while a utility table works well as a side table.

"Intricate carvings and attention to the furniture lines inspired my love of these pieces."

—MARTHA LAUREN

Vanity collections add glass and silver sparkle to a bath or dressing area. A large armoire with chicken wire doors displays collectible dishware and cookbooks alongside a rustic planter stand.

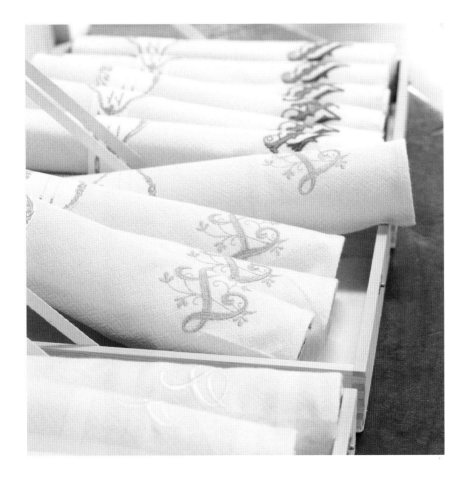

C'EST MAGNIFIQUE

BRINGING DISTINCTIVE FRENCH ÉLAN AND ELEGANCE TO ITS
THREE CALIFORNIA LOCATIONS, JAN DE LUZ TAKES CUSTOMERS ON A
EUROPEAN TREASURE HUNT WITH NO PASSPORT REQUIRED.

After Brigitte de Luz and her husband, Jan, vacationed in picturesque Carmel, California, 19 years ago, even their native France couldn't keep them away from the seaside paradise. They packed up their family and returned to stay, bringing a delightful Gallic sensibility with them. Jan's career as a retailer of fine woven linens included launching France's first écomusée—a museum celebrating Basque

weaving, history, and crafts. Now, that same style and heritage infuse the couple's three eponymous California shops, Jan de Luz, in the city of Carmel-by-the-Sea, in Carmel Valley, and in Saint Helena in the Napa Valley.

The Carmel village boutique brims with authentic French antiques and accessories featuring that *je ne sais quoi*—an understated charm possessed by timeless discoveries beautifully preserved—and handmade luxuries for the kitchen, bed, and bath. The linens carried here are still made in the old-fashioned Basque tradition, with the colors woven into instead of printed on the cloth. Olive oil pressed from the 500-tree grove on the de Luzes' property fills attractive bottles. The shop's jasmine-and-lavender soap quickly earned a place on Oprah Winfrey's annual Favorite Things list. "People told me they saw the soap on Oprah," says Brigitte, then still a newcomer to the United States. "I said, 'Oprah? What is Oprah?'"

In the charming Carmel, California, shop named for him, Jan de Luz, along with his wife, Brigitte, offers an intriguing collection of French antiques and artful accessories reminiscent of those found at an enchanting Parisian flea market. From rustic to gilt, weathered stone to marble, the furnishings, linens, tableware, and bath oils are made the Old-World way—by hand, slowly, and with the utmost care.

Customers can stroll the shop to find an ornate cachepot or vintage glassware for their castle and then drive to the Carmel Valley store to buy the castle itself. At this 40,000-square-foot location, Jan explores his other area of expertise: collecting and selling architectural materials rescued from ancient European estates. The rare finds range from Louis XVI–era mirrors to rustic butcher blocks. Hundreds of fireplaces, tiles, statues, columns, wishing wells, doors, and gates lure architects and home builders from around the country.

"Style is a lifelong grooming of one's point of view," Jan says. In his design book, *The French Touch* (Gibbs Smith), he illustrates how antiques can glamorize

The Basque linens sold at Jan de Luz are an art form in and of themselves. A popular pattern known as leiho, left, consists of a white damask field created with tone-on-tone weaving and embellished with multicolored serge stripes woven into the fabric. Hundreds of embroidery patterns can be added to customize the products on-site.

home and garden with the soothing patina of history. He delights in the way the unconventional use of old things imbues a space with whimsy and wonder.

One of his recent clients swooned over a wooden spiral staircase, marveling at the distressed banister and the indentations from a thousand footsteps. Even though the man owned a one-story house, he purchased the staircase for his living room. From behind the sofa, it now ascends to the ceiling as sculpture—an enduring testimony to old-growth forests and the skilled hands and tools of artisans past.

RESOURCES

COMFORTABLE ELEGANCE, PAGES 14-25
Designed by architect Alex Krumdieck, Krumdieck
Architecture & Interiors; 205-324-9669.
Interior design by Mary McCollister Finch, Mary McCollister
and Company; *marymcco@aol.com*, 205-907-6279.
Limestone fireplace from Architectural Heritage;
architecturalheritage.com, 205-322-3538.

RUSTIC FRENCH STYLE, PAGES 26-37
Interior Design by Mallory Smith, Mallory Smith Interiors;
205-978-9770. Cabinets, island, hood, countertops, and
chandelier by Ben Smith, Welded Wood Specialty
Products; *weldedwood@gmail.com*.
French décor from Maison de France Antiques; *facebook.com/
MaisonDeFranceAntiques*, 205-699-6330.
Barstools from Park Hill Collection; *parkhillcollection.com*,
501-603-0600.

WHERE GRACEFUL SHADOWS FALL, PAGES 56-69
Beverly Ruff Antiques and Linens, 205-262-9434.

PICTURE PERFECT, PAGES 70-83
Heather Cummans Photography; *heathercummansphotography.
com*, 205-504-1114.

NATURE AND LIGHT, PAGES 114-135
Ribbons made by Heather Cowie and Ginny Au, Froufrouchic;
froufrouchic.com.
Sketches by Edward Cowie; *edward-cowie.com*.

LE PETIT CHATEAU, PAGES 94-111
Interior Design by Frances Stanford, Maison de France
Antiques; *facebook.com/MaisonDeFranceAntiques*,
205-699-6330 and Mallory Smith, Mallory Smith
Interiors; 205-978-9770.
Built by Chris Reebals, Christopher Architecture
and Interiors; *christpherai.com*, 205-413-8531.
Arches and custom doorframes by Ben Smith, Welded Wood
Specialty Products; and blacksmith Derek Weldon,
Welded Wood Specialty Products; *weldedwood@gmail.com*,
205-229-0683.

FRENCH ELEGANCE, PAGES 148-157
Interior Design by Pandy Agnew, Pandy Agnew Interiors;
thegoodlifebirmingham.com, 205-467-0103.
Built by Scott Thomson; *scottthomsonbuilder@gmail.com*,
205-369-1800.
Painting by Emily Ozier; *emyoart.com*.

ROOTED INHERITANCE, PAGES 178-183
Landscape architecture by Jane Reed Ross; *janereedrossla.com*,
205-223-1481.

CHERISHED TREASURES, PAGES 188-197
Martha Lauren; *marthalauren7@gmail.com*, 205-516-2633.

C'EST MAGNIFIQUE, PAGES 198-203
Jan de Luz Antiques; *jandeluz.com*, 831-659-7966.